Kaj Munk

The Wartime Poems

Kaj Munk

The Wartime Poems

Despair

Those thousand years— they've taken flight
this morning five o'clock of fright.

Kaj Munk, 9th April 1940

New Nordic Press 2017

Copyright © 2017 by New Nordic Press
Translation © by Brian Young

No part of this book may be reproduced in any form or by any means without permission in writing from the publisher, except by a reviewer, who may quote brief passages in a review.

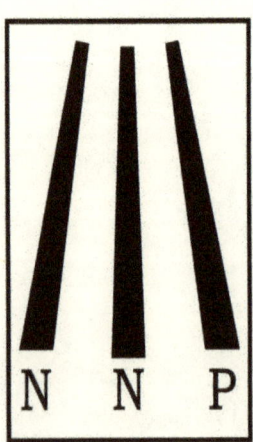

ISBN 9780989601016
LCCN 2017902292
New Nordic Press
Port Townsend, WA
www.newnordicpress.com
Cover painting by Else Young
Cover layout by Marita Sempio
Printed by Lightning Source
Printed in the United States of America

About the poems

Kaj Munk started writing poetry in grade school, and never stopped. He felt torn between the need to write, and the call of the church. He chose both. He was Denmark's pastor/poet/playwright.

With one exception, the poems in this collection are taken from the Memorial Edition of the works of Kaj Munk, published in 1949 by Nyt Nordisk Forlag in Copenhagen, in nine volumes. The volume titled *Poetry* contains 218 poems.

This collection of poems is taken from those written during the occupation, with one exception. I include Kaj Munk's first poem, written at the age of eight. The first line in that poem later became the title of his autobiography. The last line became the title of a collection of his writings and articles.

The poem given on the title page, *Despair*, was written after the evening church service, April 9th, 1940. That was the day that Germany invaded Denmark, and the long night of the occupation had begun. That poem is given again in the body of the text. The last poem, *Demotion*, is taken from " That Fate Will Not Be Ours (*Den Skæbne Ej Til Os*)," printed in 1943.

The memorial poem by Martin A. Hansen was first printed in the fall of 1944, in the illegal collection *A Flame Is Burning,* published by Folk and Freedom. It was printed without the author's name, as all such publications were strictly censored and illegal.

There are 30 poems in this collection. The first was written when Kaj Munk was eight, the next two in 1940, the following five in 1941, Hymn to the Faith in 1942, and the remaining in 1943.

About the endnotes

Mathilde Munk, Kaj Munk's youngest granddaughter (daughter of Arne & Hanne Munk) has written a short interpretation for all of the poems included here. There are also some historical references, and I urge the reader to consult these notes as they are reading the poems. They begin on page 57.

About Kaj Munk

Kaj Munk was born Kaj Harald Leininger Petersen on January 13, 1898, in the town of Maribo on the Danish island of Lolland. He lost his parents at an early age: first his father when he was just one, and then his mother when he was five. Soon afterwards he was adopted by his mother's cousin Marie, and her husband, Peter Munk. It was from them that he got his last name. They lived on a small farm in Opager, 15 Kilometer west of Maribo.

Kaj's new parents belonged to the "Inner Mission" or evangelical movement, and that would come to influence the young Kaj Munk. He was often present at "conversions" in the movement's Inner Mission house in Brandstrup, a neighboring village.

Marie Munk had decided early on that Kaj should study for the ministry. He was clearly a gifted child, and she thought that anything else would be too little for him. Kaj showed an aptitude for language, and was already writing poetry while still in elementary school. He would later find it difficult to choose between the two callings—poetry and the church. In the end he chose both, and became known as Denmark's pastor-poet. Yet he was perhaps best known for his theatrical works. During the thirties Kaj Munk was the most frequently staged dramatist in Scandinavia. He is perhaps best known outside of Scandinavia for his drama "The Word," which was adapted for the screen by Carl T.H. Dreyer in 1954, and filmed on location in west Jutland near Vedersø. Kaj went to high school in Nykøbing on the island of Falster. He enrolled at the University of Copenhagen in 1917 as a theology student, and graduated in 1924.

After graduation the time had come to find a position, and he applied for a post at the church in Vedersø in western Jutland. Kaj did not even know where the town was, and had to consult a map to find it. There were just six hundred souls in his new parish.

Kaj Munk gave his first sermon in Vedersø on New Year's Day, 1924. He would remain pastor at Vedersø until his death twenty years later, January 4th, 1944.

That was the day the Nazis would try to silence him. Denmark was in the fourth year of the German occupation, and in open revolt. Kaj Munk had been an outspoken critic of the German occupation, and an increasingly outspoken voice of the resistance. The Nazis had learned nothing about Denmark. They murdered Kaj Munk, but they could not silence him. He was taken from his home on the evening of January 4th, 1944, and murdered along the roadside near Hørbylund. His body was found the next day, and a simple wooden cross was placed at the spot. It was later replaced with a granite cross. There is no inscription on the cross. Every Dane knows whom it is for.

Kaj Munk was a beacon of light in Denmark's darkest hour. He is one of Denmark's most noted and discussed men of letters, and he remains so to this day. Although there was then, and continues to be to this day, controversy surrounding the life and the works of Kaj Munk, the fact that he grew progressively critical of the Nazi occupiers, that he refused to be silenced, and that he paid for that with his life, cannot be denied. After the war ended there was a scramble among many of those who were once willing lackeys of the German Reich to regain, or retain power in Denmark. Kaj Munk, who had been unwilling to compromise, was an uncomfortable thorn in the side of those who did—the collaborators. Revisionist historians, and those who preferred to cover their own tracks, tried to write him out of history. He was what we would today call an inconvenient person, who had spoken an inconvenient truth. But interest for Kaj Munk is alive, and is again growing in Denmark.

Brian Young, translator-editor

Port Townsend 2017

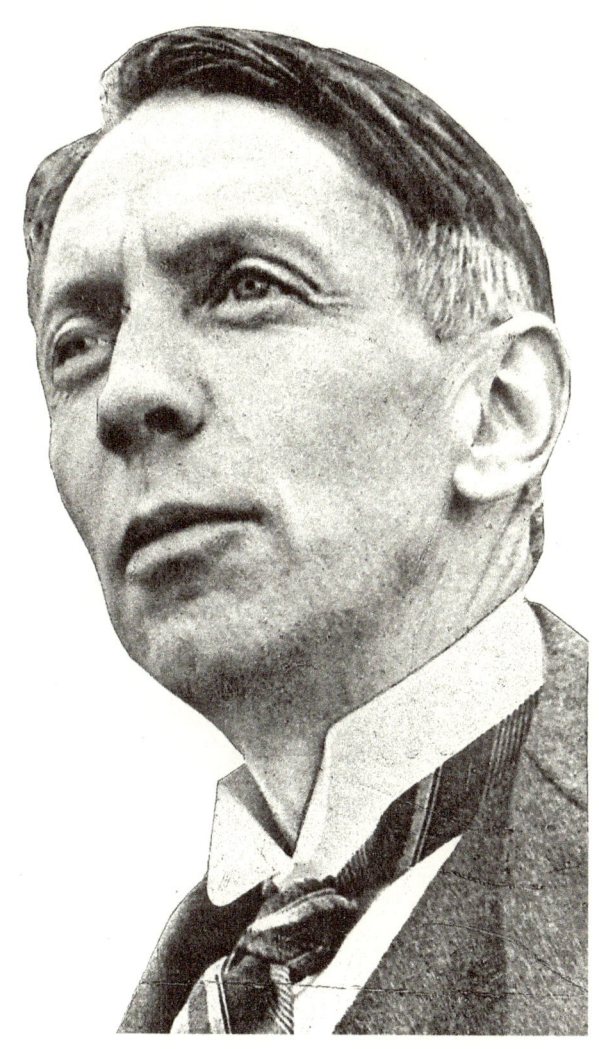

Kaj Munk

Memorial poem by Martin A. Hansen
(1909-1955)

Kaj Munk
Half a year after his death

*Listen, the cock crows in Jutland's heath,
where is my friend with the black cap?
Up, little lark, rise up and sing,
we can't see him from tuft and grass!*

*I cannot easily fly up to the clouds,
for my wings are tired and weak.
The sparrow told us, gray and sick,
in the winter they took our friend away.*

*No, we'll never hear his voice again.
But the plover, which lives in the sandy dune,
she comes now, where he is home,
and sits and sings there often.*

*But the cock calls from Jutland's heath:
Why haven't you followed the dead?*

*And gulls cry from sea to sea,
high and deep, far and wide and away,
black in the south, and dark in the north,
we cry over a victim's grave!
Time is short, time is short.
Do you all hear, on the sea and land?
Time is short, and
we are the victims' crying hearts.*

*They kicked him,
broke his face,
hit him, hurt him, twisted him,
shot lead through his head
that God had made so rich.
Murdered with vile lead his heart*

that the Creator had made great and fervent.
But you have almost forgotten that
in half a year,
sleeping countrymen.

No, rather a trip to the park,
a record on the gramophone,
and a harmless song about national unity
from a lectern that is ashamed of itself,
hung with flags that are ashamed of themselves.
No, then a trip to the woods.
No, a thousand kroner for a ride
with Germans.
Tobacco from England instead of bombs.
Amiable sabotage,
good speed for the invasion,
but not here,
just not here.

And then he was dead,
tossed in a ditch,
silent.
So they thought
they would put out his words,
but for that fire
there was not enough water in the world.

Dannebrog is not a tablecloth
for Tivoli and pancake stands,
for dishonest lecterns
to dress up every town mayor.
The victims' blood has colored the cloth,
so bold and white as the cross
was their faith.

List of poems

Kaj Munk Half a year after his death	13
So quietly comes the spring	17
An Evening Song for The Children	18
Despair	19
August	19
He drove the wailing women out	22
Lost	23
Let the light shine	24
Our Danish Call	24
Hymn to the faith	25
Denmark, our Life	26
Of Viking Blood!	27
Seawall Builders	28
The Man with the Tweezers	29
Three kinds of countrymen during war	31
"Culture"	32
We have it Pretty Good	33
The Rich and the Poor	34
Open Letter to a Secretary	35
Also him!	37
The Truth Is Growing	38
The Hidden Spirit	40

The God of every Front	42
Law is Life	44
The Flag that only lives in its coffin	47
The Eternal Caution	49
Chaff	50
The Blue Anemone	51
My Young Beloved is Throwing Up	53
The Fallen	54
Demotion	55

Kaj Munk's first poem
So quietly comes the spring

So quietly comes the spring,
soon we'll await *the glorious summer,*
where the birds live in their home of green.
They sing for us so sweet a song,
sing and chirp the whole day long,
while the grass and the flowers grow.
——Then we'll hope,
for a bountiful year,
with sun and lots of joy.

(This was Kaj Munk's first poem, written at the age of eight.)

An Evening Song for The Children

Thank you, Father, up in heaven,
Who tries to please me
Through the long and happy day.
With my cheek upon the pillow
I look up through the window,
And see your heaven's starry sky.

For you are sitting there inside,
there my prayer can find you,
It's so light and easy.
I have laughed and played,
And done so many things.
Now I am so nicely tired.

Now the mist of sleep is coming,
Will you watch over me?
While the nighttime hours pass,
You sit up there between the stars,
And watch over and take care.

And will you also be
This night with those I love,
Who now I sleep away from?
With Dad and Mom, and others,
And the King of all our land,
Yes, all of them I care for.

Then there are no others,
And there is no more to say,
Now I'm in your care.
So now we'll just say Amen,
And we'll sleep together
Until a new and lovely day.

2

Despair

Those thousand years— they've taken flight
this morning five o'clock of fright.

Kaj Munk, 9th April 1940

August

I am just the heather, not regarded well,
wherever possible, I am just turned out,
and long forgotten then, the good that I have done.

But that time man's folly
gave the oak to saw mill's teeth,
and gave up the forests to the wild sand.

When Denmark was laid bare for fate's anger,
then it was me (who no one valued),
who took up arms for our country's life and peace.

So small I was, so easy to overlook,
used to suffering disdain and scorn— but thought:
he laughs best that laughs last.

As truly as it was my home, my own country,
I knew, that what would come would come,
I stood my ground, and will continue there to stand.

And the wind shook my brown locks,
and the sand gnawed on my black roots,
but I held on, and we stood our ground.

The tall rye now no longer grew,
and the oak's giant brood on the field lay,
often where the greatest fall, the small still stand.

The angry sand I put in the lee,
and the storm that angrily blew past,
spent to no avail its rage.

If the draught was cruel to me, and the frost hard,
and evil, though not as evil as you thought,
I stood against you, century upon century.

"How barren, how ugly!" They often said of me,
but when you fight for life against all odds,
then nothing is left over for pomp.

Though ugly is not the word for me at all,
when under the mirages' ghostly knock,
I bring the coronation robe from August.

See, I fade to red, and blush to blue,
and clothe young Jutland just as well
as the Milky Way her silver train clothes heaven's prince.

Oh, grant you, busy traveler, a rest
in moss and lichen, where humble grass,
greets you with her sunny smile.

I let the thyme dance about your foot,
I let the mint's aroma touch your blood,
and hold you just for fun in moss.

While cranberry child's cheek red and round,
on the moss' pillow sweetly sleeps,
the crowberry trumpets her dreadlocks.

Wide-awake, the cowberry peeps about,
while the blueberry seeks her own reserve,
modestly in her dream's blue night's mist.

Then listen as the black grouse sings,
and splits the air like a curlew's cry,
across the hill and to heaven's height.

Forgive me that I sing my own praises.
But I really am a paradise;
at least I have the snake to prove it.

A heaven I am, —and yet,
with fire and plow and peasantry,
I shall now be put to death, be put to death.

Well, to complain had never been my style,
just let me rest a bit,
perhaps I conquered greatest, when I died.

I remember now, that there where I now stand,
was forest and field once in Denmark's land,
and in my death I dream about the spring,

When the land that I saved, my heart's poem,
when grain and trees again stand proud.
Then gladly will I die. I have done my duty.

4

He Drove the Wailing Women Out

Maybe we should be praying now,
for the storm, stinging and raw,
is coming from the world beyond.
"Dear Lord, dear sweet Lord,
Remember us, remember us,
And soothe your little Denmark.

Yes, put her on your lap,
and dry her sweet red cheeks,
and the little tears of fright.
We never would have hurt a fly,
and we didn't want to play.
How mean the big ones are!

Yes, it's a real shame for us,
just because they want to fight,
that we get interrupted in our play.
Lay our heads upon your breast,
we could use the comfort of a crib,
and a nap would be so nice.

And while we slumber in your arms,
sing us a lullaby at dusk,
one the night can never silence.
Let us awaken at the dawn,
and then we can play again.
Oh, please be nice to us dear Lord.

—Now stop that sniveling!
Don't call the Lord on high,
nor call His enemy a coward.
We're only waiting for the funeral,
so our pastor Ohsodear,
Can give a soothing sermon.

But there are no corpses here,
and gone is the armband, and the wailing,

and the mourning letters!
What's been wasted in drivel and strife,
shows now that we are full of life,
that now we want to live.

For he who can, is proud to know,
that when the test is given,
he'll be there to take it.
So let's now give thanks to God,
that this time we have been aroused,
and armed with all our might.

5

Lost

I looked at our Lord's jigsaw puzzle,
that's what I called it when I was little,
when I saw my Denmark's map,
only afraid that He could not find,
one of the pieces, if it got lost.

Was that a warning? Did that fear foretell,
the child's soul of the man's distress, now
that all is lost, in the darkness of the night?
For now—God remember us with mercy—
all the pieces have been lost.

And when I look at my childhood's map,
which once shone bright of mirth,
I see it only through a veil of tears,
and ask: Will You find it again?
Lord, will You find our land again?

6

Let the Light Shine

The night is black, and blind as death,
and we must show no light.
Then be sure, that the light in your mind
can shine, can shine, can shine.

7

Our Danish Call

Now Denmark asks of us, that we stay strong,
so that fear and doubt never will prevail.
That which threatens us soon shall learn,
that stronger yet our spirit will endure.
Only courage and strength we'll show,
where storm and sea assails our coast.
If we are few and small and weaponless,
then the more will we resist!

Now Denmark asks of us, that we stay strong,
faithful to that voice that is our Danish call.
Let arrogance and despondency know,
that the Dane has never been for sale.
Let "Gold" entice, and let the sword be raised!
Just one answer we will give, and that is no!
The white cross of sacrifice in the sea of blood,
for seven centuries has shown us the way!

Now Denmark asks of us, that we stay strong.
Let the pawns of compromise fall down!
Soon we'll gather before Dannebrog's sign,
this people who pledged its mother loyalty.
Our dear land, our proud old realm,
we'll carry you forth in the coming spring.
Let the storm rage, and the sea rise up!
Then the more our spirit will stay strong.

8

Hymn to the Faith

*So quietly it comes,
this summer of life,
despite death's frost and snow.
If never you lose faith,
then never will it fail,
that you again will see
the sunlight on the fields,
with birdsong, and
with flowers.
So the heart can freely laugh,
Then never will it fail,
that you again will see.*

*To dare believe and hope,
that is like life's fool,
to defy death's cunning.
Only humility, that understands
the difficult art to wait,
has vanquished fear.
Stand firm! Stand firm!
In gloom and sleet!
If the cold stings your mind,
and the storm rages: Then flee!
For he, with faith, that dares to wait,
he shall prevail against death's fear.*

*Of all the kinds of courage here,
Perhaps patience
is the noblest.
It is not a splendid courage,
but it has hidden strength,
against want and mockery and woe.
Let cruel and raw
the winter stay,
as out from hangmen's mouths
the triumphator laughs!*

What faith is yearning for,
shall faith then have revealed.

Denmark, Our Life

Denmark— defiled and bound!
We here have sworn an oath:
to never ask for peace,
until we have freed you,
purified and whole.

Wherever you command us,
we'll fulfill your mission for God.
Only one can command us, and
two languages only we'll speak:
Silence and Danish.

If one forgets his oath to you,
and like a coward or stooge,
grovels for a foreigner's whip —
He's the son who betrays his mother,
And we'll avoid him like the plague!

Denmark, for your freedom and honor,
we silently pledge our oath.
Onward to victorious peace,
with our death we'll free you,
Denmark, our life.

Of Viking Blood!

We've been singing long enough,
and it's been so sweet and nice,
about mom and her spinning wheel,
and dad and his old hat,
of cobwebs on the field and marsh—
as if we were a museum here.
But Denmark now demands of us
that we sing another song.

You organist with hair so gray,
you fiddlers from out west,
now we ask of you to hit those keys,
and do your very best.
Yes, sound out over Denmark's youth,
we might be children of the earth,
but are and will be, all our lives,
also children of the sea.

Small finches have had summer's fest
in the light and warmth of night.
But awaken now, you storm from west,
and blow in your bassoon!
You were a hero in heathen times,
a herald for our young free folk,
who showed us then that valor stood,
no matter how it stormed.

Our land is just a plainsman's home,
without the mountain's shelter.
Then all the more we'll lift our faith,
and our will shall be like iron!
Poor folk are often full of courage,
and often great in valor.
Show now that we have gone to fight,
that we are of Viking blood.

11

Seawall Builders

*They're building seawalls on the coast,
those quiet Jutlandic men.
The sea had taken so much land,
they'd learned to fight again.
They are small against this foe,
but they know they fight for life,
and dare to resist, although they know,
the road to victory is pain and strife.*

*He tries to calm them with rosy promises,
and friendly flatter on a summer's day.
But Jutland's men are building seawalls,
and will not wait for sunny days,
while the terrible abyss still shows its face.
But what is built holds its ground,
and when the sea draws back again,
we'll see once more our regained land.*

*So we learned in spray and foam,
our defense is to strike again.
We'll not live at the tyrant's mercy,
for we are free and valiant men.
The more he threatens,
the more we'll defy—
we build seawalls, we build seawalls,
and we'll take back what he took from us.*

12

The Man with the Tweezers

A bit thoughtless, and rather girl happy,
that always was our capital,
with winter's sunshine in it's embrace
— It's just Copenhagen.
Then suddenly appeared a dragon,
and showed its scaly wings:
"I'll search no longer now!" it said,
"For here I've found a nest."

The air was filled with sound and fury,
dripping from the swollen belly—
ruin, mutilation, death—
rained down upon the city.
The eggs fell down, the eggs fell down,
blood splattered from the sky,
flames rose up from off the streets,
as darkness fell upon the city.

Then the town was filled with eggs
from out the serpent's brood, and
Men with hoses were out in force
and battled gallantly.
Look, here's one, whole and round—
Then—"I'll just wait a second,"
was heard within its shell,
"and then I'll hatch and murder."

Then came a man with—just guess!
What do you think? A tweezers!
With which he poked about a bit,
around the hellish sneaky thing,
and finally poked it quiet.
People laughed and cried, and asked him,
how did you dare, how did you dare,
to do what you have done?"

"Well, if I was a surgeon, my friend,
and made—" he smiled as he answered—
"A small mistake with my knife,
it could cost another's life.
But if here a mistake I make,
it will only cost me mine.
So that's the best for me."
— And now on to the next!

See, old Denmark, did you doubt?
Look, there are some boys here yet!
So warm it swells within my breast,
with thanks, and blessed pleasure.
Your bard—oh yes, your journalist,
he finally saw some valor,
and tipped his hat in honor
to the man with tweezers.

13

Three Kinds of Countrymen during War

There is an old adage,
and it's not just said for fun:
that more than life what matters is,
Necesse navigare.
With those words we'll blow a kiss,
to those who sail the sea,
now in this time of war.
It's a skill the Danes know well.
What do those men, who stand so fast,
when all the seas assail them?
They sail.

We also have another sort
of countryman among us.
When things get scarce, they're on the spot,
as with a sixth sense, but
they use that sense so selfishly,
and for their own good only.
And they are seen as mainly thieves.
What do they do, when with their paws,
of long fingers search about
the counters while they point?
They steal.

But tell me— that tired crowd—
that lacks all decency,
and stands and lifts its hands up,
as if an order was given?
To disobey they do not dare,
so they surrender
for "money and for life!"
Then suddenly let out a squeal,
that rises from their throats like bile.
Tell me what they ail?
(They heil!)

14

"Culture"

A man who wears a doctor's hat
has given us the honor to ask
the question: what is culture? — And gets
for an answer: Culture is to smile, when
you would rather cry and scream.

Our earth went to its knees when a wild animal got loose.
But it finally met its fate, a people who,
instead of well-mannered smiles,
with women's tears, and man's rage,
dared to take up arms against it.

But heavenly doctor, who sees to our people,
give the Danes the cure!
Cash in the note from the doctor's hand,
and turn our pens to knives.
To lessen each day our culture.

15

We Have it Pretty Good

*What do I care if the earth
turns into a morgue?
I get my four beers a day,
and I have it pretty good.
There's plenty to do. And that's not the case
when people are not being shot to death.
So, all in all, I guess one might say,
it's my good fortune.*

*I'm not mean; I want you to know that.
But the truth is, in fact,
in peacetime it's kind of like
everyone's down in the dumps.
During a war a lot of people have it rough,
but then too a lot of people have it made.
And now that I am one of the latter—
Well? Right? What?*

*If I meet someone with a toothache,
I'll just go on my way.
Of course I wish, that we all could be
just as well off as me.
But I know that just can't be,
and I'm not a fool,
to just wring my hands in pity.
That won't help you or me.*

*No, I'm just afraid that peace
will turn us all into chumps.
Right now it just seems to be,
that all one can say is thanks.
Well, I'm on my way, and thanks for the chat,
It was nice with a little talk.
But it's bloody hell, that we have
this shortage of tobacco!*

16

The Rich and the Poor

Brother worker, yes, it's bad,
for you are not an earl.
It's by the labor of your hands
I know that you will live.
But think, if you can and will,
that work that you've been set to do!

Perhaps you have a son among
the men of the navy's pride.
Then you'd not be the one
to wound him mortally.
Then tenfold heavy your loss of son,
should you have a part in that son's death.

And remember the great birds' flight,
with death beneath their wings!
That day they come here to strike,
you know they will spare none.
I think your peace of mind would break,
if you were guilty in a landsman's death

But you, my dear director,
who keeps or casts aside,
and your soul and spirit,
for blood money sells,
what good do you think gold will do
for he who's called a traitor?

17

Open Letter to a Secretary

What you'll never understand, Mr. Secretary,
though you may be kind enough at heart,
is that a people would rather lose their lives,
than they would lose themselves.
Well, you think that's just a saying,
and you ignore it so calmly,
for you life has just one goal,
to play your cards so boldly.

Oh, you smart ones, how stupid you really are,
that simplicity must laugh at you—
you think earth's kingdom need only
one straight and easy path.
It may be good enough for the lowlands,
while the rest can be taken with tact.
But to the defiant realm of the volcanoes,
the minister has never ventured.

You can show your face,
in air that's as cool as snow.
But the heart needs to be nurtured
by a fire (that none can see.)
You call yourself a captain,
but you sail on a freshwater sea.
God save you, if it's the ocean,
and a storm should come your way.

Yes, smile sarcastically, Mr. Secretary,
and call me a peasant and fool.
But for intelligence I'd rather use
my hearts own intuition.
You are a fool to deny life's source,
and believe that it will never be,
that one day a volcano will erupt,
through all of your hesitancy.

*No, you'll never get it straight,
and you'll never understand,
that heart and blood are the color red,
while the brain is the color gray.
And Sampson will never be vanquished,
before the temple falls down,
he will kill the enemy, Mr. Secretary,
even if he must kill himself.*

18

Also Him!

Also him! Like salt in a wounded heart,
when the newspaper or the radio,
now pawns in a foreign play,
again names one who betrayed the faith,
and deserted that people he belonged to.

We read quickly, so as not to see,
and nervously turn off the radio.
Another one, we thought he was a man!
Will we be too few to set a watchman?
It's almost daily now: Also him!

—Let that which is rotten inside fail,
and that which concealed the rot.
Let the storm throughout the forest rage,
when the rotten follows life's death law,
then the more will purity endure!

19

The Truth Is Growing

Timidly, and without honor,
they turned the country over.
Even if we didn't have an army—
even if we had nothing else,
we had at least No!
And if our hands could not prevail,
then our spirit could have stood
for truth and honor on our path.

Timidly, and without honor,
they turned the country over.
Boys, take a lesson from this,
and tell them that it's not that way
that Denmark's spirit and youth will fight.
Proud men at Denmark's altar,
not cripples limping
in pathetic deceit.

Timidly, and without honor,
they turned the country over.
We can't deny complicity here;
we all swallowed the lying promises,
and bought the false sense of security.
And to continue marching
on this path will only hide
old sins and shame with new.

Danish people, you simply cannot,
in this great and fateful hour,
stand there with a blank expression,
as an irresponsible group,
pretending to be deaf and dumb,
without rejoicing, without trembling,
as in an underground vault,
as in an aquarium.

Wake up, wake up now, today!
No more refuge in your sleep!
Wake up to action and to the ruins!
Men are judged by daring.
Remember, it's your home soil.
Let them threaten, and arrest,
steal your honor, and deport.
That's how Denmark grows.

Wake up, wake up now, today!
Now it's death to sleep.
Wake up to action and to the ruins!
Men are judged by daring.
Remember, it's your home soil.
Let them threaten, and arrest,
steal your honor, and deport.
In that way the truth is growing.

20

The Hidden Spirit

We believe today in Denmark's hidden spirit.
All that we see before us
of indulgence, we don't believe,
but rather on your defiance, smiling with restraint.
We believe today in Denmark's hidden spirit.

Government, parliament, courts, police—
all that, which should have shined in darkness,
but instead was scared into a mouse hole
and helps the strangers against their countrymen.
There Denmark's spirit cannot be found.

He is snoring in his Kronborg resting place,
one believes. Another, with derision in his mouth,
that when Stauning sold the soil,
Holger Danske was part of the deal:
Our people now just want the peace of slaves.

But Holger's friends know, that that is just a lie.
We listen and look into the fog:
Yes, it's true; the old one wakens now,
and moves concealed amongst us. And day and night
we see about us his handy work.

There is a Denmark, which shall go to its grave,
That Denmark, that just to save its life,
ran headlong into a stranger's custody,
and disregards our faith and honor's call.
Praise to God: it shall go to its grave!

For such is the law: He will reach that goal,
who lifts his eyes to the horizon,
and sets a course for heaven's star.
In the swamp, only in the swamp, for him,
who runs after the swamp's night watchman.

That people who now, as through a thousand years,
had the courage to give up life for life,
and for their love have given up themselves,
that Denmark, thanks to God, we know,
will stand as long as stars 'cross heaven flow.

21

The God of Every Front

I am the Lord. There is no other.
Disarm every "power" you come before.
The air, the earth, and the sea I am God over,
I am the Lord, the God of every front.
Just believe then, that it is you who rules!
God's power is of love only.
And therefore am I the God of anger,
when you scorn the call to love

To you my heart is yearning day and night,
my children, my very dearest.
I would set you all about me,
and lead you past harm's way.
But you spit on my burning love,
suit just yourself, and only seek your own.
Have you nourished cowardice within your heart,
shameless for our enemy's bite?

If love is trampled underfoot,
then your life will turn to hell.
To no others will you listen,
then I am the God of zealousness.
Triumph then for now! Be well at ease.
As ye sow, so shall ye reap!
Take to the sword, and the sword will strike you.
Slowly I raise my heavy arm.

Defenseless towns of Abyssinia,
You, smashed along the road to peace,
while your emperor kneeled in his church,
sending prayers to the deaf arches!
Those, who sent you bombers, flee
now from their ruined homes, and scream.
He, who princes drove from their domains,
is a refugee now, back in his own land.

I am God of the air, the earth, the sea;
the God of all the fronts. I take my time,
but I heal always the wounds of justice,
and strike with my fist injustice in its face.
Mock me, kill me, and bury me so deep.
See. I stand here yet. Judgement will be mine,
and yet my time is always coming,
slowly, with the lightning of revenge.

22

Law is Life

You throw words of acid at my face,
and fearfully avoid the ace of spades.
"Your words in Denmark have no weight,
for you are enemies against our people's state."
Alas, you make a grotesque and horrible mistake,
for now it's you who fail the people's state,
fleeing from yourselves before full sail,
and me, who had so fervently foretold your fate.

Yes, before I swung down with my flail,
to beat grain to the stable floor.
And shall I live; the time will come again,
—perhaps—to strike down hard against its core.
But what we before this time could think,
you, countrymen! Oh, let's wipe away that smile.
What must now be asked is this one thing:
Where were you on the ninth of April?

We cannot stage a comedy now,
on whether democracy or dictatorship
is most expedient, or even something else.
About that we must now be as silent as a wall,
so long as the night wears down our strength,
and predators stalk an inner dissent,
where they yet can take that bite,
that their claws so long desired.

We must with love's faith and defiance
—and truth's spirit shall make it bold—
only keep that which unites us,
and, countrymen, that is the law, the law, the law.
If it is good, or bad, put that argument aside,
when those from without are no longer here within.
The law is our own, and we will set it right. For now
the law is good, for it is Danish, and it is ours.

Then stand watch about it, Danish men,
and keep your vision clear and sharp despite dark arts,
and boldly call that treason, that
which will use the law for tricks.
With that at heart in battle we shall go,
not just to save our ship.
We will, we will, that Denmark shall endure.
And rather die with honor than live without.

To die! We Christians do not believe in death,
but on the profound words from Nazareth,
that if you'll live, then this you must,
to risk all in the face of death.
We believe, that law is life, and he who betrays
life's law will rotten from within.
Life for our land is our deepest goal,
and the law without question we affirm

But, you say to me: "Easy for you to talk.
You sit so comfortably without.
A cock at roost can so easily crow.
But the time for manly action is now here.
We think: as long as we get by,
then we'll have done quite well.
To act so we get swept aside
is a reckless deed. Can that do any good?"

So then I answer you with all my might:
"I believe with all my heart it does great good."
Those ideals that you were called on to defend—
let others show them to the door.
Do not believe, that with untarnished spirit
your heart's No can turn to Yes upon your lips.
If you go hand in hand with darkness,
you will learn that it rubs off.

To want to win, and yet decline to fight
is poison for the people's soul, and fool's play.
O' blind Denmark; believe me, your rant

against the sting leads nowhere.
Here you stand at Damascus' gates,
where scales fall from off your eyes.
Then repent, give your will to truth!
Then great will be your future, and your call.

23

The Flag that only Lives in its Coffin

Why fly the flag, when you think it's just a rag? When you shirk from the vow, that is the flag's plea and its command?

To raise Dannebrog, be careful, it never is a joke.
The flag will seek revenge, if you think it's just a toy.

See, its red color swells with its call for sacrifice:
you can only love it if it is burning in your blood.

For your heart's sake let it crush your heart's arch!
For, O' man, your heart is more than just yourself.

Don't you feel the white cross of innocence
demands your mind be bright and true, so you cast your eyes down?

You, who carry a forked tongue behind your lip's smooth skin, bite one off, but quick, bite it off and spit it out!

You stand there and raise the flag, despite its soul is laid in bonds!
Do you think it's just a piece of cloth? Don't you know a flag is spirit?

Humility is Denmark's brand, yes, but never a creditor's.
Never will our hearty cross be planted in a foreign cloth.

Never shall its pure cloth be used in low comedic play,
fooling us that our freedom is still here.

Free, only free the flag shall wave— seven centuries' Dannebrog, not by another's mercy. Then rather keep it under cover.

Never share the flag with a stranger! Keep it hidden, for it is yours. In your heart its flame shall burn, warm and alive and free

Only when it has won its victory, sacrifice red, and innocent white, then that day it will wave over a people high and free.

24

The Eternal Caution

The old sick men kept up their babbling:
to save life and limb is what's important.
Even in death we heard them babbling:
"Oh, be cautious! Just, be cautious!"

And those who tried to raise the flag on high,
for truth, for courage, and for valor—
they were asked to move aside, for
it was hoped that youth would be enthused,
and this high ideal support.

This cure they fervently practiced,
with sincerity against all forms of plague.
And therefore they have finally croaked.
From what? Of course from caution!

25

Chaff

*The devil is sifting his grain.
Hear how he laughs on his loft,
casting aside with anger,
all that which is able to grow.
The chaff is his harvest, and
he keeps only that which can't live.
See how long they've been silent,
and how long flagrantly proud.*

*Yes, they're light in the wind,
flying before his shovel.
It won't be long before,
they burn in the fires of hell.
Up to heaven they'd have been blown,
but reach only the opposite goal,
to be swept, when sow time is here,
down into the fires of hell.*

The Blue Anemone

*You little anemone
How great our Maker is!*

*But what was this that happened?
My heart, though frozen hard as quartz,
would melt if it should see it,
on this, the first of March.
What broke through the deep black soil,
and with its sea blue blossom gave,
a touch of Heaven's tone?
The little anemone
I planted there last year.*

*I brought it back from Lolland,
a memory from my island home,
and then I went and waited,
and thought that it must die;
for it missed it wooded glen,
its mild air, its fertile clay;
in this hostile place
my anemone will die—
I'll see it nevermore.*

*But now it stands there nodding,
triumphant in Jutland's sandy soil.
Invincible and confidant,
despite solitude and fog,
as if the world's adversity
had given it a greater worth.
A little anemone,
and still my anemone,
like a gleam off ocean wave.*

But what was this, that happened?
My heart though frozen hard as quartz
would melt if it should see it
on this, the first of March.
I thought: "Forever now they're torn apart,
my soul and my contentment," as I sat
in winter's cruel grasp.
But now my anemone
warms my heart again.

For this pure color is,
to me a breath of spring,
and like a child, it gives to me,
an everlasting hope.
So I bend down towards the earth,
and gently stroke its flower,
a touch of mercy's throne.
You little anemone,
how great our maker is!

27

My Young Beloved is Throwing Up

*My young beloved is throwing up,
and cries: "Go! Stay away from me!"
It shakes her feeble body so.
Oh, beloved, how I care for you,
the golden sweat glistens on your brow,
and pastes your hair against it,
where oft the light danced about,
as if a halo around you.*

*When first your resistance broke,
when first you heard my heart was calling,
then in a hesitant cast of dice,
your kiss caressed my lips,
and then that night you playfully,
drew me down to your boat of longing,
and sailed with me through joy and tears,
high above the starry night.*

*How deeply I have loved you, girl of mine,
and proudly called you my little wife,
for your silver speech, and wine of thought,
for the face's beauty, and the body's flame.
But never did my heart burn so,
with fondness for you, as now—
when pale and sickly you
chase me from out your room.*

*Our happiness' living starry catch
under your belt you carry as a gift.
With all your torment, your fear and shame,
you carry an eternity within your life.
Without the fight and the defeat
none shall win his victory's day.
O' warrior for the cause of life,
I honor you more than I can say.*

28

The Fallen

Boys, you boys who died,
you lit in Denmark's deepest gloom
a shining sunrise.

Blessed Danish boys!
Our eyes are full of tears. But our hearts beat
so proud as never before.

For now we again can
look the world in the eyes,
for you saved Denmark's honor.

You gave us life again.
They tried to forbid you to use
the weapons they themselves had given.

Hail to you Viking sons,
Disobedient Danish soldiers, thanks!
May God forever reward you.

Demotion

What's this for a double man,
who's driving around in our land,
and has a lot of men with him,
who have nothing to do with this land?

He's dressed up—and not to boast—
as fine as were he a general,
and acts, no matter where he drives,
as if he was our land's director.

And the men with him,
they behave just the same.
We others think these words,
"he gotten on the wrong track."

They're driving downhill now,
with a speed that's quite alarming,
so this supremacy will end,
with a crash against a wall.

Despite being a general and director,
they drive themselves to ruin.
They'll get what here was broken down,
that fate they long deserved.

But what should Denmark do, with
that mob that caused such harm?
"When they've been taken down
then douse them with gasoline"

Yes, the young who can, say
traitors up against a wall!
O', if one could be a Vulcan.
I'm too old, and too humane.

When Denmark's mourning time is over,
then give them jobs in Tivoli.
Make the general and the director
into roller coaster ticket sellers.

30

1 So Quietly comes the Spring

"So Quietly Comes the Spring" is both the title of the boy's first poem, written at age eight, as well as the title of the Danish edition of the grown man's memoirs, which were written a few years before his death during the war, when he sensed the way things were going. There is a lot of symbolism in this poem. At a very early age, the young boy was essentially given a "death sentence" because he was so frail and sickly, that he was not expected to live very long. But life triumphed, as he writes about in his memoirs.

But the spring comes quietly and carefully in this world, and it is often difficult to believe that it can, despite all of its fragility, put an end to the cold of winter, even though we see this happen over and over. We sense it, but understand it first, when summer is in full blossom around us.

Kaj Munk was murdered on January 4th, 1944. There is always a spring we do not see with our physical eyes, but it comes so quietly anyway....

2 An Evening Song for the Children

Kaj Munk loved children. They were, for him, a symbol of life. The life that in his young days he might have found to be confusing, but that he came to love with an intense affection.

He wrote a history of Denmark in verse, and dedicated it to the sweetest of his countrymen, the children. He used to say, that he best liked children and old people, because the children came from God, and the old were going to Him.

The poem displays an unbelievable simplicity and lightness perhaps not found so clearly in other works by Kaj Munk as in this poem. One really gets the impression that it is a child's somewhat naive communication with God, who is sitting up there in His starry heaven, before he lies down to sleep.

3 Despair

Denmark has the reputation of being the world's oldest monarchy. There is a long continuity, and a long history here. Kaj Munk was very proud of this Danish identity: "God, King, and Fatherland."

When the Germans overran the country, meeting little or no resistance on that fateful day, 9th April 1940, he thought that it was a national disgrace. It was a heavy blow that he never got over. Fear cloaked history in darkness and oblivion. The only thing left was the shame.

4 August

This poem is very Danish, and probably for that reason particularly difficult to translate.

As a west Jutlander, one can sense the heath, and its scent, when reading this poem. It was written by a man with an intimate connection with the heath, a strong love for it, and a deep knowledge of it— a man who had wandered many miles through it, and who had spent many hours observing it.

As the anemone speaks for the author in another poem, here it is the heather. And here too is a strong identification with the heather. The heather is Denmark, but it is also Kaj Munk— " Perhaps I was most victorious when I died."

5 He Drove the Wailing Women Out

Most of this poem is written in a very sarcastic tone, which becomes increasingly obvious in this poem. There seems to be no need for consolation, but rather for song. But Denmark and the Danes need to be purified, and to be made aware of life's gravity. We cannot continue to play, while the entire world around us is bleeding.

In the Bible, Jesus says that He had come to cast fire upon the earth, and that He wished that it had already ignited. That became the text for the funeral sermon for Kaj Munk.

If we love with love's passion, then we must throw ourselves into the struggle for all that we hold dear—instead of moaning over our own misfortune. There is something in life that is greater than us. There is something in life that is sacred.

6 Lost

This poem is presented in a completely different tone from the previous one. There is an almost childish bewilderment, sadness, and fear in this poem. There is sorrow and pain, and a sincere question for God.

Just as children who lose their favorite teddy bear may feel completely powerless and unhappy, adults too can lose something valuable, drop it on the floor, and be incapable of putting it back together again. Maybe it has just disappeared in the night. A God is needed to find it again, to reestablish harmony and order in the world.

That is the mood expressed in this poem, where Kaj Munk relates to a child's vision of the world, because we are all, in some way, children.

7 Let the Light Shine

There was a general blackout decree in Denmark during the war. Special close fitting curtains were mandatory, so no light could be seen in the streets or roads. Denmark was an occupied country, and the allies should not be given any aid to bomb specific targets in any town.

For that reason, the night is "Black and blind as death," and of course it doesn't take much imagination to apply this to the way we think as well.

The poem ends with a plea— that a clear flame must continue to burn in one's mind, a mind that is not bound by any blackout decree.

8 Our Danish Call

This poem calls to mind a speech from a Shakespearean play before a great battle, or Mel Gibson in Braveheart. It is a call for great valor. Kaj Munk is trying to inspire himself and his countrymen to find the courage and the will to fight.

Central to this poem—and very central to the author's way of thinking— is the sentence: Stronger yet than all is spirit.

Kaj Munk was a round-shouldered, and in many ways, not a physically attractive man. But when he spoke he could captivate his listeners.

Perhaps the strongest example of this is when he spoke at the athletic school at Ollerup on the island of Fyn in July 1940. A school of highly trained athletes, who were devoted to the perfect body— but when he stood at the podium, and began to speak, it was said that you could hear a pin fall to the ground.

9 Hymn to the Faith

This poem is a beautiful continuation the boy's first poem, about the spring that comes so quietly. However, it was written towards the end of his life, in 1942, and indicates both a development as well as a continuation. He still seems to still posses the belief that spring will win over winter—over darkness, and over death.

But he had learned through his life's experiences, that this victory can often be seen only through the eyes of faith. That does not, however, make it any less real. Faith is a gift that we have been given so that we can see what otherwise is invisible, but is still just as real—perhaps more real—than that which is visible.

The poem is, as the title says, a hymn to the faith. A prayer that we will hold on to this magical and strange thing— so that we will, actually, see the arrival of spring.

10 Denmark, Our Life

There can be a variety of reasons for not living up to what Kaj Munk would call duty, which was a an important concept for him. Two things he refers to in many of the poems from the war years are: cowardice and greed.

Do we sell out the things we believe in for profit, or because we are terrified of the power we are up against? Both of these feelings are always valid.

But Kaj Munk claims that in this way, when we betray our duty, we are also betraying our own basis for existence. He calls Denmark "Our life."

"He that findeth his life shall lose it: and he that loseth his life for my sake shall find it." (Matthew 10:39)

11 Of Viking Blood

During the first years of the occupation it was common for people to attend "Song meetings." They were arrangements where up to several thousand people would meet up to share the Danish song repertoire. They were the songs that they knew and loved, about a peaceful Denmark, about the good old days. They were songs about the wheat growing in the fields, and the farmer tending his soil.

Starting in 1943, these meetings were forbidden, but in the first stanza of this poem, Kaj Munk says that maybe we shouldn't cry over that, because, although it might have seemed pretty and good, it reduced national pride to something that belonged in a museum. Those days are gone, and we cannot sing the country back to greatness and peace.

It has been cozy long enough! But now we must fight. That stubbornness which grows in the face of headwinds must blow in over us from the wild western seas, and call forth the Viking blood in our Danish veins.

(And there is probably a reference to the Allies in the "...storm from west.")

12 Seawall Builders

A common theme in Kaj Munk's writing and poetry is David's battle with Goliath. How willpower, and the power of the spirit, can again and again win over physical strength.

In this poem he tells about the taciturn west Jutlanders, who take up the struggle against the relentless sea that had stolen parts of their land, and how they, through relentless and stubborn struggle, take back what was lost.

In the second stanza he talks about "the violent dragons of the abyss", an almost Biblical description of the archenemy, the devil— he who has come to steal and destroy.

In the last stanza we see how this ancient enemy can be seen in all of the tyrants we encounter, and how we, through our faith and deeds, shall finally see the miracle: "they are vanquished, and we regain that which we had lost."

13 The Man with the Tweezers

The dragon theme from the previous poem continues in this poem. Here we see how it descends and conquers a city with it brood of lizards. Of course, the real subject is the German occupation of Copenhagen. There is peace, and tranquility, when suddenly a terrifying beast turns the town into its nest. Before we look around, the happy and contented idyll has been turned into a raging inferno, where fire (bombs) falls from the sky.

In this instance, the poem is a tribute to an officer named Einar Lund, who under a bombardment of Copenhagen in early 1943, with limited tools at his disposal, risked his life to disable a bomb that had not exploded.

The disdain for way in which people make pacts with snakes follows a thread all the way back to the fall of man. One can see what kind of misery stems from that type of alliance. There is a Christian motif with the hero, who is ready to give his life to save mankind. But that was not the end of this story. Einar Lund lived, fled to Sweden, and died in 1982. Kaj Munk praises the willingness to sacrifice. That it still exists makes life worth living—and worth dying for!

14 Three Kinds of Countrymen during War

Once again we are given a list of three types of people: People who are willing to sacrifice, the greedy, and the cowardly. Perhaps they appear more clearly in these extreme conditions? It would seem to be that way. This might be an oversimplification, and perhaps we all have these tendencies within us. But in extreme conditions there might not be room for such nuances.

15 Culture

In this poem Kaj Munk ridicules the finely polished figments of the imagination, and those who endlessly debate with each other, and their surroundings, but are so out of touch with reality, and never put their ideas in motion. It is not the brain, and flights of fantasy, that can hold up a shield against tyrants. Rather it is feelings, heart, willpower, and faith.

He finishes the poem with a prayer that the heavenly doctor will send down a cure to the people, and that it is not human wisdom, but God's word, that is sharper and more effective than any double-edged sword.

16 We have it Pretty Good

In this poem we meet Godless men who care nothing for their fellow man. There are no ideals, no empathy. They seems so completely limited and callous, that at the same time they can seem comical. Kaj Munk could evoke many different feelings in his poems. Here he evokes a smile, even though it is really tragi comical. To emphasize the insanity here, the man has only one complaint, despite being surrounded by a world steeped in blood, and that is that he is not happy with the tobacco substitute he must use. During the occupation there were many commodities that were not available, so people tried to get by with substitutes. There is no vision, no perspective. He is locked up in his own little reality. It is an interesting poem in the way it describes the tendency toward increased isolationism that was so prevalent at the time.

17 The Rich and the Poor

There were many Danes who worked with the occupation forces to build that which was called "The Atlantic Wall"— a line of defense for Germany, erected along the European west coast from Norway to Spain, including, of course, the entire length of Jutland's west coast. Many of these concrete bunkers can still be seen, although many have been washed out to sea, or blown up due to the danger they posed for tourists swimming in the area.

Kaj Munk spoke out forcefully against aiding the Germans in this activity. It was, after all, voluntary.

He thought that God would forgive those poor farmers who "needed" the work to put bread on the table, but he asks them, in this poem, to think about how much misery and death that these bunkers would bring to others. The bunkers were, of course, built to shoot down airplanes, and bombard ships, that came from the allies to attack the German army.

In the last stanzas of the poem he attacks the rich, who contributed to this work, even though they did not need the money. He compared them to Judas, and asked them to remember, that his wealth did not save him from the terrible end that he finally met.

18 Open Letter to a Secretary

Politicians in the so-called Danish Unity government were, according to Kaj Munk, driven by common sense, and fear. They were thinking about how they best could take care of the country's interests, and at the same time look after themselves.

But some compromises, taken in the name of common sense, are deadly for any life. You cannot do violence to that which is innermost in a people, to a people's love of their country, to their desire to defend it, and to fight for their own identity, without causing something to wilt and die.

So, do we end up doing a disservice to our nation? And what is it for a people—what is it for a nation— that it survives on such a basis? What is it that survives? To survive in an amputated form is, after all, not the same as to live.

19 Also Him!

In this poem we can sense both pain and fear. We hear the indescribable sorrow over the list of "comrades" becoming shorter and shorter. Now yet another one has betrayed his country, betrayed his honor and duty. One can say that Kaj Munk ends the poem by saying that it would be better to be forced back into the catacombs, with the true message, than to maintain the illusion that the masses are accepting a message that they do not, in their hearts, believe.

Let fall down, that which cannot stand! It is better that the truth be revealed, than to live a lie.

20 The Truth is Growing

Kaj Munk has expressed this idea in other places: "The truth is not simply to believe something. The truth is to believe something, and to be faithful towards it!" This is essential for Kaj Munk— a belief without action is dead, as written in Jacob's letter.

When we are faced with challenges and trials in life, then we will see what we really believe in, and what are merely empty words.

The poem is a plea to Denmark's youth to show what they have in their hearts of love for the fatherland— and to show that the politicians have made a mistake when, through caution and cooperation, they would safeguard the nation, but instead end up taking away its life.

21 The Hidden Spirit

This poem is much like the previous one. The legend of Holger Danske is much like the legend of King Arthur in England. He awakens, when the country is in danger, and will fight for its existence and survival. Holger Danske is a stone sculpture with a long beard and sword He sits under the casements at Kronborg castle in Helsingør, "Hamlet's castle," waiting.

Kaj Munk is saying that Holger Danske has awoken, and wanders among his people, even while the Unity government seems to think that he is still sleeping peacefully, buried under centuries of history.

One is reminded of the Royal Air Force's motto—Per ardua as astra— through perseverance (The fire) to the stars. That is how it is for those who think greatly, with a holy fire in their heart. The others follow the will-o-the-wisp, the little politicians, and end up in a quagmire

22 The God of every Front

As with many of his other poems and works, this one is full of Biblical references, and Christian symbolism. There are elements from the Book of Psalms, from Isaiah, and of course from Jesus himself, who cries over Jerusalem and its fate. Our Lord is a jealous God— Our God is a consuming fire. Perhaps God seems silent, but He watches with justice over that world that He had created, and man's evil doings do not escape His retribution. One cannot despise love, and mock all that is holy, or make pacts with the devil, without consequences. God does not take sides with one nation against another. God is with all of His children. He looks into their hearts, and hears the cries of the innocent. And that is why he is the God of all the fronts

23 Law is Life

Kaj Munk was not an absolute admirer of democracy, and during the 30's the "strong men" of Europe fascinated him. That should be seen as an expression of his distaste for parliamentarianism, and for talking things to death.

Kaj Munk had been called both a Nazi and a fascist, but in truth he was never an ideologist. Ideologies meant nothing to him—they were simply mental gymnastics. But he did admire the loner.

This poem is about how the nation should unite, put aside the internal divisions, and make a united front against the foreign powers that had occupied the country. There is no time for wasteful recriminations, but only for honor and heroic action. Even if you do not believe it will make a difference, the poet says, it will always pay to listen to the truth. He compares Denmark's situation with that of Paul at the gates of Damascus, where he was converted.

24 The Flag that only Lives in its Coffin

The Danes really love their flag, and it waves high above the small cottages where people enjoy themselves with beer and pastries.

In this poem Kaj Munk says that he does not think much

of these outward shows of nationalism that have little real substance. They are just like the song meetings mentioned earlier.

For him, the flag is almost sacred. According to legend, it fell down from heaven in Estonia during a battle in 1229, and the white cross and the red background symbolized Christ and the blood of martyrs. It should not be flown as if it was just some laundry hung up to dry, in an attempt to maintain the illusion that all is well, when you are not even willing to fight for it.

No, the real symbolism of the flag will grow in the people's hearts, and when it can again wave freely.

25 The Eternal Caution

It is well known that one can overdo things in life, but it's also true that one can do too little.

In this poem, Kaj Munk is saying that one can die from being too cautious, and in a way he is correct. Because something dies, or gets strangled, and stagnates.

The poem is biting sarcasm when he talks about "The lofty ideal of taking care of oneself". It is directed at the Unity politicians.

26 Chaff

Once again we see the Biblical language, which permeates so much of Kaj Munk's poetry—and even more so, the underlying concepts.

If we are not in league with God, then we must be in league with his opponents. What we do may seem sensible, and correct, it may look like the road to success. But it is barren, and in the end can only lead to suffering, death, and eternal misery.

There are probably none of us that would want to go to our graves, knowing that we were only the chaff that gets blown away by the wind, or ends up in the fire.

27 The Blue Anemone

This is probably the best known, and most loved, of all of Kaj Munk's poems. It can be found in the strangest connections, and Vedersø, Kaj Munk, and the Blue anemone are inextricably bound together.

It is also a war poem, and a symbol of the growing resistance. But it is about more than just the occupation during the war. It is about life's unconquerable courage. One cannot fail to see how Kaj Munk's own life is reflected in the poem, and this is emphasized in the last stanza: "How great our maker is." Kaj Munk identifies himself with this poem.

28 My Young Beloved is Throwing Up

Life was sacred to Kaj Munk. He loved children. The idea of fertility control, or abortion, was horrible to him. He once said that women are most beautiful when surrounded by their children.

The poem pays homage to women— homage to the mystical union between a man and a woman that brings forth life, homage to motherhood.

It ends with a broader perspective: Woman is a warrior for life itself, where no one is victorious without struggle and defeat.

[29] The Fallen

This poem is short and concise. It is one of the best known of the wartime poems by Kaj Munk in Denmark. It was written as a tribute to those few Danish soldiers who refused to abandon their posts, or to surrender without a fight at the border, when Denmark was occupied on April 9th, 1940.

Later it became a symbol for all of the Danish resistance fighters, and it has been chiseled into the granite base of the statue at the Memorial "Mindelunden" in Copenhagen, which was where many young Danes gave their lives for Denmark, executed by the Nazis.

[30] Demotion

Pride goes before a fall, and nothing in this world lasts forever.
Kaj Munk tells here a story about how this fall can appear, and about the vindictiveness that often accompanies the fall of the great. But, as he explains in this poem, that does not always, automatically, return order to the state of things.

The satisfaction of seeing people get "what they deserve" is one thing. But what of the cause itself? When the great are brought down, Denmark is still in the same position. And to punish with flame and fire might be something that appeals to the young, but Kaj Munk felt that he himself was too old for that stuff. A fitting punishment could well be that the fallen were given some simple job in Tivoli, a Danish amusement park.

After the war German soldiers were forced to search for landmines in the dunes. They were forced out to search with no safety precautions, and nobody cared if they lost life or limb. There was probably a sense of cruel satisfaction to see the occupiers, even though one had cooperated with them earlier, put, without mercy, in harms way. They had, after all, laid out the mines themselves. I believe that Kaj Munk would have spoken out against this, if he had lived.

The granite cross at Hørbylunde

Works in English by and about Kaj Munk

Five Plays by Kaj Munk Translated from the Danish by R.P. Keigwin
Nyt Nordisk Forlag Arnold Busck 1964, The American Scandinavian Foundation
Contents: Herod the King; The Word; Cant; He Sits at the Melting Pot; Before Cannae.

Niels Ebbesen by Kaj Munk
Translated into English by Arense Lund with Dave Carley
December 2006 (straight translation and an adaptation)

Niels Ebbesen: Historical Drama in 5 Acts: Translated from Danish by Erna Voight and H. Orlo Miller
The Scandinavian News, Sept. 1942-Feb. 1943

Christianity and Resistance in the 20th Century
From Kaj Munk and Dietrich Bonhoeffer to Desmond Tutu, Brill 2006

Kaj Munk: Playwright, Priest and Patriot,
Translated and edited by R.P. Keigwin
The Free Danish Publishing Company, 1944

Scandinavian Plays of the Twentieth Century
Princeton University Press, The American Scandinavian Foundation, New York 1944;

The Honourable Justice, translated by R.P. Keigwin, 1952

Egelykke
A drama in five acts, translated by Llewellyn Jones, 1954

Modern Scandinavian Plays
Strindberg, August, New York,
Liveright Pub. Corp. 1954, Including Kaj Munk's play Egelykke.

Swans of the North: and short stories by modern Danish authors, by Heepe, Evelyn, G.E.C. Gad, Copenhagen 1953, comprising Kaj Munk's: But it's not like him!

By The Rivers of Babylon
Kaj Munk – 15 sermons, Translated by John M. Jensen
Lutheran Publishing House
Blair, Nebraska 1945

Four Sermons
by Kaj Munk, Translated by John M. Jensen
Lutheran Publishing House
Blair, Nebraska 1944

Kaj Munk and Germany
Søren Daugbjerg, Aalborg University Press 2008
Translated by Brian Young, New Nordic Press 2011

By the Rivers of Babylon
The Wartime Sermons of Kaj Munk
Translated by Brian Young, New Nordic Press 2013

Works in Danish used for this translation:

Kaj Munk—Mindeudgave—Digte
Nyt Nordisk Forlag Arnold Busck, 1949

Den Blaa Anemone af Kaj Munk
Ringkjøbing, A. Rasmussens Bogtrykkeri
1943 (udsendt i 300 eksemplarer)

Sværg Det, Drenge
Nyt Nordisk Forlag, 1945

Den Skæbne ej til os
First printed in Ringkjøbing 1943
Reprinted by Nyt Nordisk Forlag 1969

Kaj Munk's Sidste Digte
Frit Nordisk Forlag
København 1944

Kaj Munk
8 nye digte
Forlaget Norden
Aalborg, Januar, 1944

www.ingramcontent.com/pod-product-compliance
Lightning Source LLC
Chambersburg PA
CBHW051713040426
42446CB00008B/860